Donna Higgins

NOTE TO PARENTS

This familiar Bible story has been retold in a sensitive and simple way so that young children can read and understand it for themselves. But the special message of the story remains unchanged. It is the message of God's love and care for us all.

Copyright © 1988 World International Publishing Ltd.
Revised text © 1994 Kenneth N. Taylor.
All rights reserved.
Published in Great Britain by World International Publishing Ltd.
Published in the United States by Tyndale House Publishers, Inc.,
Wheaton, Illinois.
Printed in Germany.
ISBN 08423-1292-7
01 00 99 98 97 96 95 94
9 8 7 6 5 4 3 2 1

A Boy Helps Jesus

Retold by Marjorie Newman
American edition, revised by Kenneth N. Taylor
Illustrated by Edgar Hodges

Tyndale House Publishers, Inc.,
Wheaton, Illinois.

One morning long ago in Galilee a boy woke up very early. This was the day he had waited for. This was the day he was going fishing! He got out of bed, got dressed, and ran out of the house.

Carefully, he scrambled out over the rocks. He peered down into the water and slid his hands in gently. *SWISH!* The boy brought his hand out with a fish. He tried again. *SWISH!* He caught another fish!

The boy tried again and again, but he could only catch two fish. On his way home, he passed some boys who teased him. "You only caught two fish," they said, laughing.

The boy paid no attention to them. His mother didn't laugh. She put the fish in the oven to bake. But just as they were ready for him to eat, the boy heard something.

People were hurrying past the house. Some of the boy's friends were there.

"Hey!" they called, "Jesus is up on the hillside! We're going to see him!"

"Please, Mother, can't I go, too?" the boy asked.

"What about your fish?" his mother asked.
"Please can I take the food with me?" he begged.

"All right," his mother said. Quickly she packed the fish and some bread. The boy took his fish and bread and ran to catch up with his friends.

The boy and his friends hurried along the hillside path. Now there were crowds of people, all going to see Jesus.

"There's Jesus!" one of the boys yelled as they finally reached the hillside. The boy and his friends pushed through the crowd so they could see better.

Then Jesus began to speak.

He taught the people many things about God, the loving Father. He told wonderful stories. And he healed the sick.

Later in the afternoon, the boy suddenly felt hungry. He had been so busy listening, he had forgotten about eating! So had everyone else. The boy started to unpack his food.

Then he heard one of Jesus' friends say, "Master, it's late. The people have had nothing to eat. Send them away now. Then they can buy food in the nearby villages."

Jesus answered, "Go ahead and feed them.
Jesus' friend Philip looked surprised. "But it would cost lots of money to buy enough for all of them!"

The boy thought about sharing his fish. *But I'm so hungry!* he thought. *And my small fish could never feed so many people.*

He looked down at the two fish. He remembered how the boys had laughed at him that morning. Perhaps Jesus would laugh, too.

The boy looked again at Jesus. No, Jesus wouldn't laugh.

Shyly, the boy went forward. He touched Andrew, another of Jesus' friends. "Here is some food!" he said.

Andrew smiled at the boy. He took him to Jesus. "Master!" he said. "Here is a boy with five loaves of bread and two small fish!" Then Andrew sighed. "But what good will this do? There are so many people here!"

The boy waited to see what Jesus would do.

But Jesus smiled at the boy and accepted his gift. He said to his friends, "Tell everyone to sit down."

When everyone was seated, Jesus said a thank-you prayer to God for the bread and fish.

Then a wonderful miracle happened. The more Jesus divided the fish and the bread, the more there was left! Jesus' friends began to pass the food around to all the people. There was going to be enough for everybody!

Now the people were laughing and talking and eating! Jesus and his friends and the boy ate, too.

And when everyone had had enough, Jesus' friends picked up TWELVE BASKETS of leftovers!

The boy could hardly believe it! Jesus had done a miracle!

It was nearly dark now. The boy set out for home with the other people from his town. He couldn't wait to get back.

He rushed indoors. "Mother, Mother!" he shouted. "I have to tell you what Jesus did!" And he told her the whole story.

The boy thought about all that had happened that day. It had been a day of surprises and miracles. It had been a very special day indeed!